Original title:
Cedar Screes Inside the Phoenix Cobb

Author: Daisy Dewi
ISBN HARDBACK: 978-1-80562-725-8
ISBN PAPERBACK: 978-1-80564-246-6

The Transformation of Roots

In the twilight's gentle hush,
Roots awaken from their sleep,
Stretching forth, they dare to brush,
Promising the earth to keep.

In secret soils, they twist and turn,
Whispers dance where shadows lie,
Fingers reach for warmth and yearn,
Beneath the watchful moonlit sky.

Through tangled dreams, they voyage far,
Chasing light with daring grace,
A network strong, a living scar,
In every nook, a hidden trace.

From murky depths, a splendor grows,
Woven deep, a heart in bloom,
With every drop, a story flows,
A tapestry beneath the gloom.

The roots entwine with hope ignites,
Defying storms with steadfast might,
For when the dark meets morning light,
A world anew shall take its flight.

Glimmers of Hope Amongst the Ashes

Amidst the ruins, life dares to bloom,
In shadows deep, dispelling the gloom.
Tiny sprouts push through the gray,
Whispering tales of a brand new day.

Each flicker of green, a promise to mend,
As nature's hand begins to extend.
The warmth of the sun ignites the ground,
In the heart of the ashes, hope is found.

Lament of the Transformed Woods

Once vibrant forests, now hushed and bare,
Whispers of sorrow hang heavy in the air.
Ancient trees, with branches torn,
Cry silent tears for the lives they mourn.

In shadows long, the echoes of change,
Fleeting glimpses of beauty, now estranged.
The canopy weeps, a muted song,
In the heart of the woods, something feels wrong.

Phantoms of the Charred Canopy

In the sky where once life danced,
Now shadows linger, dreams expanse.
Ghostly forms of what used to be,
Hanging quietly from each blackened tree.

The sun filters through, a ghostly light,
Illuminating stories of the night.
Phantoms whisper soft, a haunting refrain,
In the silence of loss, echoes remain.

Nature's Resilient Resurgence

From the depths of ruin, life takes a stand,
With tenacious roots, it reaches the land.
Little by little, the ground starts to shift,
A testament to time and nature's gift.

Color returns, where gray was once laid,
Fields of wildflowers, bright and unafraid.
Nature's strength, a powerful guide,
Through trials of fire, she will abide.

A Reverie of Celestial Growth

In the twilight's gentle embrace,
Stars weave tales in silken space,
Dreams of blossoms, fresh and bright,
Grow with whispers of the night.

Moonbeams dance on silver streams,
Cradling softly woven dreams,
A serenade of hope and might,
Nurtured under starlit light.

Wisps of smoke in the cool air,
Secrets linger everywhere,
From the earth, new life will spring,
In the dawn's warm, welcoming wing.

Gentle breezes carry sage,
Each petal turns a sacred page,
Nature's brush paints every hue,
A canvas fresh, a world anew.

Through the roots, the stories flow,
In silent thickets, secrets grow,
The reverie of shadows cast,
Whispers of the future, vast.

Echoes of Verdant Flames

Amidst the glades, the hearth ignites,
Crimson hues in quiet nights,
Whispers crackle, spirits rise,
A dance of life beneath the skies.

Flickering lights in emerald sheen,
A legacy of what has been,
Olden tales of joy and dread,
In every ember, hope is fed.

Green leaves sway, the fire bends,
Where earth and sky, their message sends,
Bathed in warmth, the cool night air,
Contentment blooms where hearts lay bare.

Nature's rhythm, fierce and sweet,
With every pulse, our hearts repeat,
A chorus grand, both wild and free,
In nature's arms, we yearn to be.

From ashes rise the feathery ferns,
Each cycle teaches, each season learns,
Echoes linger, fade and grow,
In verdant flames, the memories flow.

The Enchanted Remnants of Nature's Fire

In the heart of night, secrets glow,
Whispers of ages long ago,
Softly glowing, a tree's desire,
Breath of life, nature's fire.

Crimson petals, ashes dance,
Woven tales of fate and chance,
Mystic shapes in shadows lie,
Breath of earth, a silent sigh.

Twinkling stars above take flight,
Guardians of the quiet night,
Each flicker tells of paths once trod,
The remnants speak of earth and her prod.

Echoes of love in every leaf,
Fragments of joy, lessons of grief,
A cycle spun in twilight's grace,
In every corner, we find our place.

With every breath, the world conspires,
To remind us of our deepest fires,
The remnants live, forever thrive,
In enchanted woods, dreams come alive.

Rebirth in the Heart of the Wood

In the cradle of trees, time stands still,
Nature whispers, a gentle thrill,
With tender roots entwined in grace,
Life awakens in this sacred space.

Misty mornings greet the dawn,
With the promise of rebirth drawn,
Each sunbeam warms the sleeping earth,
As nature hums her song of birth.

Squirrels dance on branches high,
Chasing shadows, they flit and fly,
A symphony of joys untold,
In the heart of the forest, bold.

Ferns unfurl with gentle sighs,
As life unravels 'neath azure skies,
With every pulse, the wood will sing,
The cycle of life, a precious thing.

Through tangled paths and silent glades,
Each creature shares the life it shades,
In the heartwood's deep embrace,
Rebirth flourishes at nature's pace.

Fables in the Fiery Whisper

In shadows deep, the tales unfold,
Of whispered winds and hearts of gold.
The ember tales of nights long past,
In fiery glow, their legends cast.

A candle's flicker, the stories soar,
Of heroes brave and ancient lore.
With every spark, the fables weave,
In whispered tones, they never leave.

Through misty paths, the echoes call,
Of gallant deeds in the twilight's thrall.
A dance of flames, where dreams ignite,
In every cautious step, delight.

With vibrant hues, the canvas shows,
The artistry of life that glows.
Each flicker warms, each shadow plays,
In whispered tales, the heart obeys.

And from the ashes, wisdom springs,
Like woven roots of magic wings.
In fiery whispers, bonds entwined,
Fables forever, in hearts, enshrined.

The Phoenix's Heartbeat

In dawn's embrace, a firebird sings,
With every pulse, the promise brings.
From ashes cold, it lifts its head,
In vibrant colors, love is fed.

With a fierce heart, it lights the way,
Through tempest storms and skies of gray.
In swirling flames, the dreams arise,
A dance of hope beneath the skies.

The heartbeat echoes, pure and bold,
A legend known, a tale retold.
With each rebirth, the spirit flies,
In fiery light, the old world dies.

Beneath the scorn, the flame does grow,
Through darkest nights, its ember glow.
In every heartbeat, passion's flight,
Resurrected in the depth of night.

And so it soars, above the fray,
In brilliant hues, it finds its way.
The phoenix dances, fierce and free,
In flame's embrace, eternity.

Awakening in the Wake of Fire

From distant echoes, voices rise,
In the scent of ash and painted skies.
Awake, the spirits call once more,
In fire's wake, they dance and soar.

With flickering warmth, the heart ignites,
Through tangled dreams and starry nights.
A whisper soft, a gentle plea,
In ardent waves, forever free.

Embers swirl in a vibrant show,
A tapestry of light that grows.
With every pulse, the dreams align,
In paths of fire, their souls entwine.

And from the glow, the courage stirs,
In flames that twist and twirl like furs.
Each spark a beacon, shining bright,
In fire's embrace, they find the light.

Awakening now, anew they rise,
In fiery whispers, ancient ties.
Together forged in blazing art,
In the wake of fire, a brand new start.

Nostalgic Branches of the Blazing Sky

Beneath the branches, stories grow,
Through autumn leaves, in brilliant glow.
The blazing sky holds dreams untold,
Of whispered secrets, soft and bold.

In twilight's grace, the colors fade,
Yet in their dance, sweet memories laid.
A gentle breeze, the past returns,
In every flame, a heart that yearns.

With every branch that sways and bends,
In nostalgia's warmth, the soul transcends.
The blazing sky, a canvas vast,
Of intertwined futures and shadows cast.

The sun's embrace, a fleeting kiss,
Of vibrant dreams, the endless bliss.
With grateful hearts, we find our place,
Beneath the branches and fiery space.

As twilight falls, the stars appear,
In every twinkle, a whispered cheer.
Nostalgic branches, memories high,
Forever dancing in the blazing sky.

A Tapestry of Fractal Ash

In the sky, the embers dance,
Threads of fate in fiery chance,
Woven dreams of ash and flame,
Whispers soft, yet so much claim.

Patterns swirl on every breeze,
Nature's craft, a sweet unease,
Each fragment tells a tale anew,
A past alive in ashes' hue.

Silent echoes swirl around,
Lost moments lying on the ground,
Fractal forms of life once bright,
Now cradled in the soft moonlight.

Faded glory, yet a spark,
Life from death, ignites the dark,
In every grain, a story spun,
A dance of shadows, now begun.

Through the night, their voices rise,
In the stillness under skies,
A tapestry of what once was,
In fractal ash, a sacred cause.

Reflections of the Forest's Spirit

In the glade where silence breathes,
Nature's spirit softly weaves,
Shadows flicker, soft and bright,
Murmurs dance in fading light.

Each leaf whispers a timeless lore,
Rooted deep in ages' core,
A mirror to the soul within,
Where the forest's tales begin.

Rippling streams like silver threads,
Tracing paths where beauty spreads,
In gentle sighs, the woods convey,
Lessons whispered through the day.

Among the boughs, a secret hum,
An ancient hymn that calls and thrum,
Reflections of a world so vast,
Echoes of both present and past.

With every rustle, every sigh,
The spirits linger, never shy,
In every nook of leafy green,
The essence of magic yet unseen.

Flickering Hues of Forest Spirits

In twilight's shade, the colors glow,
Flickering hues that ebb and flow,
Secrets shared in softest light,
Dancing forms that take to flight.

With whispers sweet, they beckon near,
Echoes of what we hold dear,
Every shade, a story spun,
A world alive, where dreams are won.

Through tangled vines, where shadows leap,
Forest spirits softly creep,
Moonlit paths where wonders gleam,
Reality intertwined with dream.

Their laughter weaves through murmured leaves,
In every heart, a song believes,
Flickering forms that shift and sway,
In the heart of night, they play.

And when the dawn begins to break,
Their presence fades, yet hearts awake,
For in our dreams, they find a home,
In every soul, they ever roam.

Phantoms Among the Burnt Boughs

In the silence of a charred remain,
Phantoms dance in lost refrain,
Among the boughs, so still they sway,
Echoes of a brighter day.

Ashen whispers fill the air,
Lingering such tales of care,
Life once danced in colors bold,
Now a memory, dark and cold.

With every step through scorched terrain,
Joy and sorrow intertwine in pain,
Ghostly forms in twilight's gaze,
Haunting songs of past displays.

Echoes ripple, shadows blend,
Silent witnesses, they attend,
In the burnt remains, they find their place,
Amongst the ashes, love's embrace.

Yet with each breath, hope flickers bright,
From burnt remains, we see the light,
In every heart, a spark ignites,
Phantoms telling of new delights.

Ascending from Ashen Petals

In shadows where the flowers fell,
A whisper weaves through time's soft knell.
From ashes rise the hues once bright,
A tapestry of day and night.

With every breath, new life awakes,
In every heart, a journey shakes.
The petals dance, a fragrant breeze,
In harmony with stirring trees.

Though trials etched in seasons past,
The spirit's flame forever casts.
A spark ignites in twilight's glow,
As dreams ascend, and courage grows.

Through winding paths of emerald shade,
Where laughter echoes, fears do fade.
The ashen past, a canvas bare,
Is painted bright with hopes laid bare.

In every bloom, a story told,
Of battles fought and hearts of gold.
Together wrapped in nature's care,
We find our strength, our spirits rare.

Voices of the Restored Wilderness

In forests deep where silence sat,
The whispers stirred in softest chat.
Each rustle spoke of life reborn,
Where dreams of old were brightly worn.

The rivers sang with crystal tones,
The ancient rocks, they turned to bones.
In harmony, the creatures come,
Their fleeting echoes softly hum.

From crumbling hearths, the wildlings tread,
Awakening the dreams long dead.
Through tangled vines, they weave their song,
A symphony where all belong.

The winds do cradle tales of yore,
As nature's breath unlocks the door.
In every shade, a voice proclaims,
The timeless dance of life remains.

With open hearts and arms outstretched,
The wilderness, anew, is etched.
In unity with every life,
We forge a path, dispelling strife.

The Haven of Eternal Ember

Beneath the stars, the embers glow,
A warmth, a light in depths of woe.
In whispers shared 'round fireside,
Hope flickers bright, a cherished guide.

The hearth, a place where stories weave,
Of dreams pursued, of those who believe.
With gentle care, the sparks ignite,
A world reborn in flickering light.

From ages past, the flames arise,
A tapestry of truths and lies.
In every flicker, echoes call,
The strength to rise, the will to fall.

As shadows dance in twilight's hue,
Together forged, the brave and true.
In every heart, the ember stays,
A beacon bright through life's wild maze.

So gather close, let stories blend,
In the haven where our souls mend.
Through every trial, we stand as one,
With eternal embers, the journey's begun.

Remnants of a Fiery Legacy

In ashes gray, the tales do sleep,
Of fires burned and promises deep.
Memories linger, shadows cast,
A reminder of glory past.

With every flame that flickers bright,
A legacy shines through the night.
For every loss, a lesson learned,
In every heart where passion burned.

From smoldering ruins, arise the brave,
To forge their paths, their spirits save.
The spark within, a guiding flame,
Emerging strong and free, untamed.

Through history's veil, the voices call,
Of those who dared to rise and fall.
In reverence, we carry on,
With fiery hearts, forever strong.

So let us honor what remains,
The spirits whisper through the plains.
In every ember's gentle glow,
A legacy we nurture, sow.

Beyond the Ashen Canopy

Beneath the thick, ashen veil,
Whispers of dreams still prevail.
Glimmers of light peek through,
Dancing on hope, ever true.

Through the shadows, courage grows,
Carried by winds, the spirit flows.
A path emerges, bright and bold,
Stories of legends, long foretold.

With every breath, the forest sighs,
Embers awaken, reaching the skies.
The heart of the woods, a sanctuary,
Guardians dwell, wild and free.

Time stretches thin beneath the boughs,
Each second a spell, a timeless vow.
Together in silence, we embark,
Lost in the forest, igniting the spark.

As dusk falls, the stars appear,
Holding the wisdom, ever near.
Beyond the canopy, dreams ignite,
In the embrace of endless night.

A Story Beneath the Layers of Green

In the heart of the ancient wood,
Where stories echo, deeply understood.
Layers of green weave a tale,
Of every creature, every trail.

Moss carpets the ground, soft and bright,
Cradling the dreams that take flight.
Beneath the branches, secrets hum,
A symphony whispered, a delicate strum.

Following paths where wildflowers bloom,
Each petal a memory, dispelling the gloom.
The tapestry rich, with life intertwined,
In shadows and sunlight, wisdom combined.

Time dances here, in cycles of grace,
Every heartbeat, a hallowed space.
Nature's embrace, both fierce and kind,
Beneath the layers, the world intertwined.

With every step, a story unfolds,
In this green realm, where life's tales are told.
Forever I wander, lost yet found,
In the embrace of the earth, profound.

Ascent of the Rejuvenated Kindling

Once dulled by the shadows of despair,
A flicker emerged, casting glimmers rare.
The breath of the forest, warm and wise,
Kindling hope, where the old flame lies.

Rejuvenated spirits reach for the sun,
As branches sway, the dance has begun.
Life finds a way, resilient and strong,
In the heart of the forest, where we belong.

Amidst the ashes, new shoots arise,
In a symphony whispered through the skies.
With each crackle, a promise is made,
From the depths of the earth, a renegade.

The ascent is steep, but courage thrives,
In the embrace of the wood, the heart survives.
Rooted deep in the soil's embrace,
We rise together, a celestial race.

As we kindle the fire, old and new,
A dance of rebirth, ever so true.
In the glow of the embers, futures are bright,
Ascending together, into the light.

The Enigma of Fire and Earth

In the stillness where fire and earth meet,
A riddle unfolds, both bitter and sweet.
Heat dances lightly, a flickering flame,
While roots interlace, wild and untamed.

With every crackle, a secret is spun,
Of chaos and calm, the battle is won.
Fires of passion, of longing, of grief,
Buried beneath, the longing for relief.

The earth cradles dreams, both fragile and bold,
In whispers it shares all the stories of old.
The ash and the ember, both woven as one,
From darkness to light, we rise with the sun.

In the flicker, a glimpse of the soul,
A journey of yearning, a quest to be whole.
As life cycles through, the dance is divine,
The enigma ignites in this intricate design.

So gather 'round, as the fire burns bright,
And ponder the mysteries woven in night.
For in every spark, a lesson is found,
In the embrace of the earth, where dreams are unbound.

Nature's Palette in Ember Shades

In twilight's hush, where colors blend,
The russet leaves to the branches send.
A canvas stretched, where shadows play,
The warmth of dusk steals time away.

With painted skies of fiery hue,
The whispering winds in soft adieu.
Each stroke of light a tale unfolds,
In nature's grip, the heart beholds.

From golden fields to emerald glens,
The world aglow as daylight ends.
With every sigh, the embers glow,
A fleeting dance in twilight's show.

The leaves like candles in the breeze,
Embrace the night with gentle ease.
Their rustling song, a sweet refrain,
A symphony of ember's gain.

So let us wander through this dream,
Where colors meld and shadows gleam.
In every step, a breath of fate,
In nature's arms, we celebrate.

Pioneers of Resilient Green

From cracked concrete, life does rise,
With roots that grasp the painted skies.
Through every storm, they stand so tall,
These pioneers who dare to call.

In whispered winds, their secret found,
The tenacity beneath the ground.
With every leaf that greets the sun,
A tale of hope has just begun.

Through urban jungles, wild and free,
They carve a path, plant seeds of glee.
In every crack, a chance to see,
Resilient spirits, bold as can be.

The cities hum with nature's voice,
In harmony, they weave their choice.
Through every struggle, life will thrive,
In every heart, they keep alive.

So heed the call from leaf and sprout,
For in their growth, there lies no doubt.
Together we can make a change,
With pioneers to rearrange.

Eternal Dance of Flame and Leaf

In every flicker, stories burn,
As flames embrace the leaves that turn.
A waltz of heat, a fervid night,
Where shadows linger, hearts take flight.

The ember's glow, a soft romance,
Entwined together in a trance.
Their beauty bright, a fleeting spark,
A dance of life ignites the dark.

Through seasons change, this bond remains,
In whispered winds, in summer rains.
Each twirl a promise, each sway a song,
As nature sings where hearts belong.

The cycle turns, yet they hold tight,
In unity, they chase the light.
From leaf to fire, their spirits soar,
An endless dance forevermore.

So watch the dance of flame and leaf,
In every moment, find the grief.
Yet from the ashes, life begins,
In nature's arms, the dance of sins.

The Fire-Kissed Woodlands' Lullaby

Beneath the boughs where shadows weave,
A lullaby of night conceived.
With whispers soft as morning dew,
The fire-kissed woodlands beckon you.

As crickets sing their twilight song,
In harmony where hearts belong.
The embers flicker with gentle grace,
A cozy warmth in a tranquil place.

Each rustling leaf holds tales untold,
Of ancient woods in dusk and gold.
A serenade from roots below,
In nature's closeness, time moves slow.

So listen close, let worries stray,
For woodlands hum at end of day.
In every breeze, in every sigh,
The fire-kissed woodlands' lullaby.

With starlit skies and secrets deep,
The woodland dreams in silence keep.
In nature's lull, we find our rest,
In woodlands' heart, we're truly blessed.

Whispers of the Ember Grove

In twilight's hush, the whispers call,
Of secrets held in shadows tall.
The ember grove, where wild things roam,
Each flicker speaks of tales unknown.

The trees, like guardians, stand so proud,
Beneath the glow of a starry shroud.
Their branches sway, a dance of fate,
In every crackle, hearts await.

A breeze breathes soft through leaves of gold,
Unfolding stories, quietly told.
Where magic stirs in every sigh,
And dreams take wing beneath the sky.

The fireflies weave a shimmering song,
In this warm realm, where we belong.
With every step, the chorus grows,
As ember light in darkness glows.

So linger here, where sparks ignite,
In whispers of the approaching night.
The ember grove, a sanctuary,
Embracing souls, forever free.

Ashen Wings and Evergreen Dreams

In a world where shadows blend and sway,
The ashen wings drift far away.
They dance on whispers born of grace,
In evergreen dreams, their rightful place.

Each feather holds a tale of old,
Of battles fought, and hearts bold.
With every beat, they forge a path,
In the tapestry of nature's wrath.

Beneath the boughs where silence reigns,
The magic pulses through the veins.
Emerald canopies form the sky,
While ashen wings begin to fly.

In fluttering forms, they weave around,
The echoes of a soft, profound sound.
Dreams take flight like stars above,
In the twilight air, the whispers love.

So close your eyes and hear the call,
Of ashen wings through shadows tall.
Embrace the dreams that drift and sway,
In the dance of night that guides the day.

Beneath the Canopy of Phoenix Flames

Beneath the canopy, fierce and bright,
Phoenix flames set the woods alight.
A symphony of heat and light,
Guides the lost through the endless night.

The leaves, ablaze with vibrant hue,
Whisper wishes that come true.
Each flicker sparks a tale anew,
Of hearts reborn, of love that's true.

In fiery embers, dreams take flight,
As shadows yield to radiant light.
Wild voices rise, a rippling song,
Echoing where the brave belong.

The night sky glows with colors rare,
While tales of magic fill the air.
In this sacred grove, fears unfurl,
Embracing all who dare to whirl.

So dance within the flames' warm kiss,
And lose yourself in this sweet bliss.
Beneath the canopy that ignites,
Awaken dreams in starry nights.

Shadows of a Fire-Kissed Forest

In shadows deep, the forest breathes,
Where fire-kissed enchantments tease.
With each flickering light that sways,
A gentle magic softly plays.

The trunks, aglow, hold whispers sweet,
As secrets dance on silence's feet.
Among the leaves, a story weaves,
Of ancient dreams the heart believes.

Through tangled roots, the shadows creep,
Guarding lore the forest keeps.
Each crackle shares a timeless song,
Binding the weak, the brave, the strong.

In twilight's embrace, the tales align,
Of creatures born of fire and vine.
With every spark, a glimpse is shown,
Of magic's realm, where hearts have grown.

So wander forth in twilight's glow,
Embrace the shadows, let them flow.
In this fire-kissed forest, find,
The essence of a loving kind.

Beneath the Canopy of Rebirth

In whispers soft, the leaves do sway,
Where shadows dance in shades of gray.
Beneath the boughs, new lives take flight,
A world reborn from depths of night.

The brook sings sweet, a gentle tone,
As dreams revive and seeds are sown.
With every breath, the forest thrums,
A symphony of life becomes.

The fern unfurls, a vibrant hue,
In sunlight's kiss, the earth breaks through.
Each petal whispers tales untold,
Of magic spun from threads of gold.

From branches old, the spirits gleam,
In twilight's glow, the stars redeem.
A tapestry of hopes and fears,
Where laughter mingles with our tears.

So wander forth, let shadows guide,
Through paths of green where dreams abide.
For in the heart of nature's loom,
Lies the promise of endless bloom.

Flickers of Memory in the Sylvan Mist

In morning's blush, the mist unfolds,
A canvas vast with stories told.
With every step, the echoes call,
Beneath the boughs, we rise and fall.

The brook's soft murmur shares a tale,
Of lovers lost and ships set sail.
In every breeze, a ghostly trace,
Of laughter lost in time and space.

The deer appear, shy silhouettes,
In shadows deep, where nature frets.
And with each glance, a memory stirs,
Of whispered dreams and ancient verses.

Through tangled roots, the whispers flow,
From heart to heart, the stories grow.
In sylvan depths, we find our way,
Through dawn's embrace and twilight's play.

So linger long in the tranquil mist,
Where time stands still and dreams persist.
For in the woods, we come to see,
The flickers of our history.

The Winding Path of Forgotten Trees

On winding ways, the ancients stand,
With secrets held in weathered hands.
Their gnarled limbs, a timeless art,
That whispers truth to every heart.

Beneath the canopy of green,
The stories weave, though rarely seen.
In twilight's glow, the shadows creep,
Guarding dreams that dare to leap.

The mossy stones recall the past,
In nature's hold, our thoughts are cast.
With every turn, a journey bold,
Through whispered tales of clay and gold.

As gentle sighs from branches sway,
We find the strength to seek the way.
With each step firm, we breathe anew,
A winding path of trust imbued.

So heed the call of emerald halls,
Where nature's grace in silence calls.
In every rustle, every breeze,
Lie echoes of the verdant trees.

Flames of Renewal in the Green Enclave

In emerald depths, where wild things grow,
The flames of change begin to glow.
With every spark, the light ignites,
A dance of life in starry nights.

The earth awakens, stirs alive,
With fervent hope, the heart will thrive.
In flickering flames, the shadows play,
A promise bright of a new day.

The roots dive deep, they clutch the ground,
While dreams take flight; their wings unbound.
In every blaze of verdant hue,
The past dissolves, the future's rue.

As sparks embrace the dusky sky,
We find our strength, we learn to fly.
With hearts ablaze, we step and soar,
Into the light forevermore.

So let the flames of renewal burn,
For through the fire, we shall discern.
The green enclave, a sanctuary,
Where life ignites, forever free.

Timeless Roots in Blazing Ash

In ancient woods where shadows lie,
The roots entwine, they reach for sky.
Amidst the ash, where embers glow,
Life whispers soft, in tones of slow.

Each branch recalls a tale of yore,
Through storms and fire, they stand once more.
In every burn, a lesson found,
Timeless roots in sacred ground.

The phoenix rises, bold and bright,
From charred remains to glorious flight.
A dance of life, in vibrant hues,
Awakening dreams from fiery snooze.

The winds they carry songs of past,
In swirling ash, the die is cast.
With every gust, a story spins,
From swirling fire, a spark begins.

And so we gather, hand in hand,
With roots as strong, we'll take our stand.
Through fire and frost, through joy and pain,
We'll rise anew, like sun after rain.

New Growth from Old Embers

From cinders cold, a seed takes flight,
In darkness deep, it finds the light.
The past ignites, a fierce embrace,
With every breath, we find our place.

Soft whispers call from ashes grey,
A promise blooms to chase decay.
Emerging green, the hope renews,
While old embers share their views.

Each tender shoot, a story spun,
In every leaf, the battles won.
Against the odds, the journey grows,
In every heart, the ember glows.

The dance of life, relentless, bold,
In shifting soils, our dreams unfold.
When darkness fades, and shadows flee,
We find our strength, we dare to be.

With hands in earth, we toil and mend,
Finding hope in every bend.
From ashes deep, a legacy,
Of growth, of life, eternally.

The Canopy's Veil of Rebirth

A tapestry of green unfurls,
As sunlight spills in golden swirls.
The canopy, a shelter wide,
Holds secrets of the forest tide.

In whispered breaths, the branches sway,
Each leaf a dance, a soft ballet.
With every rustle, stories weave,
Of days gone by, what we believe.

Beneath its guise, the heart beats strong,
In shadows deep, where souls belong.
From every fall, new life will rise,
In emerald shades, beneath the skies.

The veil of time, a gentle shroud,
In whispered paths, we stand so proud.
For every bloom, a world reborn,
From every dawn, the night is shorn.

Within this realm, we take our breath,
In love and loss, we conquer death.
For through the branches, light will stream,
A canopy where hearts can dream.

Resilience in the Heart of Ashes

In the heart of ashes, courage reigns,
Through trials faced, we feel the chains.
Yet from this darkness, light will spill,
Resilience whispers, with iron will.

Each scar a story, etched in pain,
In barren lands, we learn to gain.
Through fire's wrath, we rise anew,
With fire turned soft, and skies so blue.

The earth is scorched, but hopes ignite,
With every dawn, we claim our right.
To blossom forth, in vibrant ways,
From deep despair, we craft our days.

As ash drifts down on whispered breath,
We weave our dreams from rags of death.
In unity, we stand and strive,
Stronger together, we shall survive.

Through storms that rage, and trials deep,
In heart of ashes, our dreams we keep.
Resilience born from all we've lost,
We'll rise again, no matter the cost.

Whispers of the Ancient Grove

Beneath the ancient boughs so wide,
Soft whispers drift on the evening tide.
Secrets linger in the air,
Echoes of magic, most rare.

A moonlit path where shadows play,
Guides the lost who seek their way.
Each rustle tells a tale untold,
Of dreams and legends, brave and bold.

The roots entwined, a sacred knot,
Guarding visions the world forgot.
A gentle breeze, a fleeting sigh,
Lifts the heart, as spirits fly.

In twilight hours, enchantments weave,
A tapestry, for those who believe.
To walk these woods, a timeless quest,
In whispers, find the soul at rest.

As dawn breaks over the emerald sea,
The grove reveals its mystery.
With each footstep, magic wakes,
In this ancient world, the heart partakes.

Ashen Echoes Amongst the Boughs

In twilight's glow, where shadows blend,
Whispers ride the gathering wind.
Once bright flames now softly fade,
Ashen echoes in the glade.

The charred remains of stories told,
Of bravery and hearts of gold.
Beneath the canopy, still they sigh,
Memories cling like a lullaby.

Stars peek through the smoky veil,
On the night's breath, secrets sail.
Amongst the boughs, a faded spark,
Illumines paths once lost in dark.

The nightingale sings an ancient tune,
To the light of a silvered moon.
Each note a tale, of hope and pain,
As ashes mingle with the rain.

With every step upon the ground,
The echoes of their strength resound.
Through the shadows, truth takes flight,
As hearts unite under the night.

Enigma of the Timber Spirit

In the heart of the forest, shadows blend,
Where time and nature gently mend.
An enigma cloaked in twilight's grace,
The timber spirit finds its place.

With branches weaving tales of old,
Of adventures brave and legends bold.
Echoes whisper on the breeze,
Unlocking doors through ancient trees.

A flicker of light, a startled sigh,
As fireflies dance beneath the sky.
The spirit calls with a haunting tune,
Beneath the watchful, watchful moon.

Through tangled roots and tangled dreams,
The magic flows in shimmering streams.
Every rustle stirs the soul,
Unveiling truths that make us whole.

In silence deep, the wisdom grows,
As nature's secrets, softly flows.
To wander here is to embrace,
The spirit's dance in this sacred space.

Shadows Dancing in the Ember Light

In the ember light, shadows sway,
Dancing softly, night turns to day.
Flickers of gold where stories burn,
In this haven, for hearts that yearn.

The fire crackles, a gentle sound,
As whispered dreams from embers bound.
Each glowing spark a wish takes flight,
In the warmth of this enchanted night.

Through swirling smoke, faces appear,
Figures of loved ones, ever near.
Their laughter echoes, a timeless song,
Reminding us where we all belong.

The dance of shadows, a sacred art,
Embraces each weary, wandering heart.
In the flickering light, we find our way,
Guided by love that won't decay.

As dawn approaches, fire's glow fades,
Leaving behind the night's charades.
Yet in our memories, the warmth remains,
In shadows dancing, love sustains.

A Symphony of Rustling Leaves

In the hush of a golden dusk,
Whispers weave through ancient trees.
Each leaf a story, softly husked,
Dancing with the evening breeze.

Crimson hues and amber flames,
Nature's music swells and sways.
Echoes of the wild's past claims,
Guiding dreams through autumn's ways.

Beyond the wood, the shadows play,
Crafting tales in twilight's glow.
Yet in the depths, the heart will stay,
Finding peace in what we know.

Rivers sing in gentle streams,
Painting paths beneath the sky.
A symphony of whispered dreams,
As the world bids night goodbye.

So let the leaves their secrets share,
For every rustle tells a tale.
In the thicket, hope is rare,
Yet in the silence, we prevail.

Dreams in the Wake of Desolation

In the barren fields of grey,
Whispers of the past arise.
Faded dreams, like ghosts at play,
Haunt the echoes of the skies.

Yet through the cracks in shattered clay,
Seeds of hope begin to sprout.
In the shadows, come what may,
Life stirs softly, without doubt.

Each tear that falls holds magic's key,
To bloom where despair once thrived.
The heart beats on, relentless glee,
In the ashes, we survive.

From desolation, dreams take flight,
Painting worlds with vibrant hues.
In the darkness, find the light,
With every breath, new paths to choose.

So lift your gaze and dare to see,
The beauty in the broken land.
Rise up, embrace what's meant to be,
For rebirth is at our command.

Whirlwinds of Renewal in the Forest

Beneath the canopy so wide,
Whirlwinds dance through verdant leaves.
Nature's pulse, a rhythmic tide,
Whispers secrets that it weaves.

Each branch a canvas, life anew,
Vibrant colors burst and blend.
In every storm, a promise grew,
Renewal where the wild woods mend.

Through tangled roots and whispered light,
Creatures stir from slumber deep.
In the heart of day and night,
The forest breathes, its dreams to keep.

Time wanders slowly, yet it flies,
Every leaf a fleeting chance.
In whispers soft, the wind defies,
Spinning tales of nature's dance.

So let the whirlwinds carry forth,
A symphony of life reborn.
In every corner, find your worth,
As the day greets the gentle dawn.

The Hidden Heart of Regeneration

In the depths of shaded glade,
Lies a heart both fierce and bold.
Through trials, the earth has laid,
Beauty in the cracks unfolds.

From the ruins, songs arise,
Echoing through time's embrace.
Nature's tears become the prize,
Nurturing a tender space.

The roots entangle, intertwine,
Finding strength in hidden seams.
Life persists through every line,
Weaving through our waking dreams.

From the shadows, light will gleam,
A testament to what we find.
In every cycle, hope will stream,
New beginnings, intertwined.

Hold the vision, watch it grow,
In the silence, listen close.
The hidden heart will surely show,
The magic in life's sacred prose.

Secrets Among the Embered Twigs

Amidst the whispers of the trees,
The secrets dance upon the breeze.
Each ember glows with tales untold,
In hush of night, their dreams unfold.

With shadows flickering in the dark,
Mysteries ignite, a glowing spark.
Beneath the canopy, secrets sigh,
As starlit wonders weave and fly.

The twigs embrace the night's sweet air,
Guarding stories hidden with care.
In every crackle, a voice prays,
To hold the past within their gaze.

The forest breathes, alive, awake,
It pulses gently, softly quakes.
In this sanctuary, spirits twine,
With every ember, they intertwine.

So listen close, beneath the moon,
For in the silence, hearts attune.
The secrets of the embered night,
Guide wandering souls towards the light.

Sylvan Soliloquy at Dawn

Awake the forest with gentle light,
As dawn breaks softly, shunning night.
The leaves unfurl, a tender plea,
In sylvan whispers, wild and free.

The brook begins its playful run,
A symphony beneath the sun.
Each note a word, each splash a tale,
In nature's arms, where dreams prevail.

The creatures stir, the world ignites,
With vibrant colors, morning delights.
As sunbeams kiss the morning dew,
The sylvan heart beats bold and true.

Among the ferns, old secrets rise,
In tranquil sighs, the forest lies.
A soliloquy on emerald stage,
Where every flicker writes a page.

Listen closely, the woods will share,
A timeless story, beyond compare.
In every rustle, a heart's refrain,
The dawn and forest sing again.

The Phoenix Nestled in Arboreal Embrace

In branches high, where dreams entwine,
A phoenix rests, a blaze divine.
With feathers bright as morning's song,
In arboreal arms, where hearts belong.

The echoes of past flames ignite,
As twilight casts its dusky light.
Through whispered winds, the tale's retold,
Of rebirth, courage, and hearts bold.

Nestled deep in emerald sheen,
The creature sleeps, a slumber keen.
In stillness, magic swirls and crests,
A promise held within its nests.

The canopy cradles every sigh,
As ancient leaves drift gently by.
In every branch, a story spun,
Of fire, hope, and battles won.

Awakened dreams embrace the dawn,
In flames anew, the spirit's drawn.
A phoenix rises, wings unfurled,
In nature's grasp, it finds its world.

Beneath the Hoarfrost and Ashes

In winter's grip, where silence lies,
Beneath the frost, the whispers rise.
Ashes crumble, memories cling,
To hidden dreams that softly sing.

The hoarfrost paints a crystal veil,
A fleeting picture, pale and frail.
But in the cold, a warmth persists,
As shattered hopes embrace the mist.

The ground, a tapestry of time,
Where shadows dance, both dark and prime.
Each flake of frost, a gentle touch,
A tender hush that speaks so much.

In stillness, buried secrets wait,
To break the ice at dawn's soft gate.
From ashes sprout new vows and plans,
A quiet promise from the lands.

So tread with care, for underneath,
The strength of life, a stolen breath.
Beneath the hoarfrost, whispers soar,
In hidden hearts, forevermore.

The Resilient Heart of the Old Grove

Beneath the branches wide and strong,
A spirit whispers of a song,
With every bark and weathered leaf,
The tales of time, both joy and grief.

In twilight's hush, the shadows blend,
Roots intertwine, where stories bend,
The resilient heart beats slow and true,
Embracing life, in every hue.

Through storms that roar and tempests rage,
The grove stands firm, a timeless sage,
With every spring, rebirth it sees,
In gentle sway of dancing trees.

When twilight falls and dreams take flight,
The crescent moon sheds silver light,
Illuminating paths once lost,
In nature's arms, we count the cost.

For in each ring, a secret held,
Of whispered hopes that nature swelled,
The resilient heart, forever will
Beat in the old grove, calm and still.

Echoes in the Smoky Canopy

The mist entwines with branches high,
As echoes weave through the sky,
Whispers dance in smoky trail,
Where memories of old prevail.

In morning light, the shadows play,
A symphony of bright and gray,
Leaves shimmer like forgotten dreams,
Floating softly in silver streams.

Each rustle tells a tale untold,
Of hearts once brave and spirits bold,
The canopy, a sanctuary,
Where echoes breathe and set us free.

As twilight wraps the world in blue,
The stars emerge, a brilliant view,
In chilled air, the past ignites,
In smoky whispers, soft delights.

And so we roam, beneath the trees,
The echoes linger in the breeze,
A tapestry of lives once lived,
In smoky canopies, we forgive.

Love Letters to a Forgotten Tree

Beneath a sky of azure hue,
I carve my heart, a love so true,
Each letter etched in bark divine,
Whispers of yours, whispers of mine.

The roots beneath, entangled tight,
Hold secrets shared in starry night,
The branches sway, a gentle sigh,
As time drifts softly, passing by.

With every leaf, a story grows,
In sunlight's warmth, the spirit glows,
Forgotten tree, it's you I see,
In every shade, you comfort me.

The seasons dance, a rhythmic beat,
In your embrace, my heart's retreat,
With autumn's brush and winter's chill,
Love letters whisper, time stands still.

Though tides may rise and winds may howl,
Your strength remains, the quiet growl,
Forever cherished, steadfast, free,
My love for you, old, forgotten tree.

The Dance of Ash and Sap

In twilight's glow, the embers gleam,
A tale unfolds, like woven dream,
The dance of ash, a fleeting grace,
As nature's hand spins time and space.

With every crackle, whispers rise,
Of ancient truths, beneath the skies,
Sap flows like time, a gentle thread,
Binding life and love, once fled.

Through seasons change, the stories blend,
In rhythmic sway, the trees ascend,
They twirl in dusk, a fervent trance,
In smoke and light, they weave their dance.

As dawn arises, colors blaze,
The world awakes, in amber haze,
In silent reverie, they stand,
The dance of ash, the touch of hand.

So here we gather, lost in lore,
With every step, we yearn for more,
To celebrate the sap and ash,
In nature's arms, our hearts will clash.

The Tree-Talker's Story

In the heart where whispers play,
A tree stands tall, old as the day.
Its roots deep in secrets sewn,
It tells of paths the winds have blown.

A voice like leaves in gentle breeze,
Recalling tales the earth sees.
Of wanderers lost, yet found anew,
In the arms of nature's view.

Underneath the starry dome,
The tree calls softly, 'Welcome home.'
In shadows dance, a spirit free,
This ancient sage, a friend to me.

It shares its wisdom, old and wise,
In quiet rustles, under skies.
Each knot and burl holds a fable,
Of love and loss, the heart is stable.

So listen close, when night does fall,
For secrets whispered, one and all.
The tree-talker speaks to hearts that roam,
In every echo, we find our home.

Dreaming Among the Fiery Pines

Beneath the sky of twilight's hue,
Among the pines, a dream ensues.
They flicker bright, like burning flames,
In whispered winds, they call our names.

Each needle tips with golden light,
A beacon glows, guiding the night.
In every rustle, secrets bloom,
A world aglow, dispelling gloom.

With every breath, the magic swells,
In the heart of woods, where silence dwells.
We dance in shadows, hopes take flight,
Dreaming among the fiery night.

The moon weaves spells through branches tall,
As starlight kisses, and echoes call.
In dreams woven with jeweled thread,
Among the pines, our spirits tread.

A sanctuary for soul's retreat,
Where heartbeats pulse in rhythmic beat.
Together wrapped in nature's grace,
We find our dreams in this sacred space.

A Haven Amidst the Scorched Earth

In fields where ashes softly lie,
A spark of hope begins to sigh.
Amidst the flames and charred remains,
Life stirs beneath the open plains.

From beneath the soil's bitter crust,
A green shoot rises, strong and just.
It dreams of rain, of skies so blue,
A haven found, for me and you.

Through sorrow's grip and shadows cast,
The spirit's song will hold steadfast.
A garden grows where few would tread,
With fragile blooms that dance instead.

In every crack, a life anew,
The heart of nature pulls us through.
With roots that dig through fire's song,
Together we learn to grow strong.

A haven built on scars and pain,
In each rebirth, we break the chain.
Amongst the scorched, a path we find,
To rise again, with hearts aligned.

When Green Meets Gold

In the summer, where whispers play,
Fields of green in bright array.
Sunlight dances on the leaves,
A symphony the heart believes.

Golden rays pierce the emerald hue,
In every light a spark anew.
Where green meets gold, a promise sings,
Of charming tales and hopeful things.

Through whispering branches, dreams take flight,
In twilight's glow, enchantments bright.
The world awakens, colors blend,
A canvas stretched, where illusions mend.

We wander through this painted scene,
When laughter twirls in spaces green.
A gentle breeze carries the tune,
Of joy that lights the waning moon.

In this embrace of life's delight,
When day meets dusk, and falls to night,
We find our place, our story told,
In the union of the green and gold.

Phoenix's Cry in the Forest's Embrace

In the stillness where shadows play,
A phoenix calls at the break of day.
Feathers of ember in twilight blend,
A fiery song that the morning sends.

Among the trees where whispers dwell,
Mysteries ring like a soft, sweet bell.
The heart of the forest begins to glow,
As secrets untold in the breezes flow.

Glimmers of gold in the dew-kissed dawn,
A dance of light where the darkness is drawn.
With each note sung from a throat of flame,
The spirits rise, never to be the same.

Branches sway to a rhythm divine,
As life unfurls, in nature's own line.
A symphony born of the earth's soft sighs,
Binding the world with the phoenix's cries.

Luminescence Among the Ruins

In the heart of stone where time has slept,
Phantoms linger, their secrets kept.
Moonlight dances on crumbled stone,
Whispering tales of what once was known.

Through arches high where shadows leer,
Stars peek in with a glimmering cheer.
Each crack and fissure a story to tell,
A haunting echo, a silent bell.

In the ruins where the wild things creep,
Nature's embrace begins to seep.
Vines entwined under skies so clear,
Casting a spell that draws us near.

Find the luminance in dusk's soft hue,
A beacon of hope in shattered view.
Past and present entwined in strife,
Illuminating the echoes of life.

Icarus in the Woodland

In a glade where the sunlight spills,
Icarus dreams on the crest of hills.
Wings of wax bask in the warm embrace,
Longing to touch the wide-open space.

The winds whisper secrets of flights untried,
Through rustling leaves where ambitions bide.
With every flutter, a heart takes wing,
Hoping for joys that the skies might bring.

Yet shadows loom in that radiant light,
Whispers of caution in the heart's flight.
The sun's waning flame a warning call,
But the woodland beckons, enticing the fall.

Each pulse of nature within him swells,
Stories of daring that the twilight tells.
To rise above, to soar, to dive,
The spirit persists, eager to thrive.

A Serene Heart Amidst Turbulent Skies

In the hush of dusk, where shadows blend,
A soft heart whispers, ready to mend.
Beneath the tempest, a calm takes hold,
A story of courage quietly told.

Clouds may roar with thunderous might,
Yet deep within, there's a flicker of light.
Harmony brews in the chaos around,
Where magic of peace can always be found.

Above the fray, where the storm meets the breeze,
The spirit of hope dances with ease.
In every raindrop, a promise lies,
A serene heart against turbulent skies.

With each breath drawn in the wild, fierce air,
Resilience blooms, stripped of despair.
For in every tempest, the stillness can grow,
A testament true to the strength we sow.

Whirlwinds of Green and Gray

In the forest's heart, shadows dance,
Leaves whisper secrets, in a trance.
Gray clouds gather, a storm takes flight,
Silent creatures slip into night.

Branches sway, a tempest's sway,
Whirlwinds beckon, come what may.
Nature's palette, rich and wild,
Under the hush, wonder's child.

Moss-covered paths, where dreams collide,
Gentle streams sing, a lullaby's guide.
Emerald hues and shadows play,
A world alive, in green and gray.

In twilight's glow, the colors blend,
Echoes of magic, around the bend.
A promise whispers in the air,
Of life reborn, beyond despair.

So let the winds weave tales anew,
Of courage found in every hue.
For in the dance of storm and calm,
Life's beauty sings, a healing psalm.

The Old Sentinel's Lament

Beneath the vast, star-speckled sky,
Stands the old sentinel, watching high.
With gnarled branches, he tells the tale,
Of whispered winds and storms that hail.

Once a lush green, full of might,
Now he stands, clad in silver light.
Every ring a memory held tight,
Of seasons passed, in day and night.

Roots entwine in the earth so deep,
Guarding secrets that shadows keep.
In silence wrapped, he weeps for all,
The fleeting moments that gently fall.

The world moves on, yet he remains,
A guardian of both joy and pain.
His echoes linger, softly float,
In every breeze, a heartfelt note.

So stand a while, and listen, dear,
To the whispers of the ancient seer.
For in his sorrow, wisdom flows,
In every heart, the old sentinel knows.

Blossoms in the Wake of Flames

In the ashes where shadows lay,
New life stirs, in bright array.
Blossoms rise from torched remains,
A testament to nature's gains.

Golden petals kiss the sun,
In the aftermath, life's just begun.
Soil enriched by fire's embrace,
A cycle completed, nature's grace.

Hummingbirds flit from bloom to bloom,
A vibrant dance dispels the gloom.
Each flower a flame, bright and bold,
Stories of strength in colors told.

Through trials faced, resilience grows,
In every heart, a spark bestows.
So let us weave our tales in light,
From darkness rises, endless flight.

In the wake of flames, hope appears,
In the blossoms, laughter clears.
A reminder found in every hue,
That in the struggle, life breaks through.

Ashen Echoes of Nature's Resilience

Amidst the charred remains of fate,
Hope flickers on, refusing to abate.
Silent stories in the soil reside,
Of strength and courage that won't subside.

Each charred tree, a tale of time,
From ashes birthed, the climb sublime.
The earth exhales, its gentle breath,
A dance of life, defying death.

Pine sap drips, a nectar sweet,
New roots find hold where old ones greet.
In shadows cast, bright colors bloom,
Nature's canvas, dispelling gloom.

The wind carries whispers, soft and clear,
Of battles fought, yet hearts sincere.
With every ember, every sigh,
The spirit of life shall never die.

So let us honor those who stand,
In the face of loss, hand in hand.
For from the ashes, we shall rise,
Nature's resilience, a grand surprise.

Where Flames Kiss the Forest Floor

In twilight's grasp, the embers glow,
The whispering winds begin to blow.
Cinders dance with potential flight,
As darkness folds the fading light.

Amidst the ash, new dreams ignite,
Where shadows waltz with hope's delight.
The floor, a canvas of charred earth,
Bears witness to the cycle of rebirth.

Brighter days will soon arise,
Through cracks of soil, lift weary sighs.
Each flame that sings a song of pain,
Sows the seeds of life again.

The flickering light plays tricks on sight,
Illuminating all that's right.
In every ember, stories weave,
Of those who perish and those who leave.

So let us gather around this fire,
And from its warmth, let hearts aspire.
Where flames kiss the earth's deep root,
New wonders blossom, bold and astute.

Silhouettes of the Reborn Trees

In the crisp dawn, shadows arise,
Silhouettes dance beneath the skies.
Old trunks lean against the breeze,
As whispers hum through ancient leaves.

Their branches stretch, a daring plea,
To touch the sun, to be set free.
With every bough, a tale unfolds,
Of love and loss, of courage bold.

Roots entwined in stories past,
Stand steadfast, eternally cast.
In twilight's cloak, they sway and bend,
A promise held that trees will mend.

The forest breathes, a rhythmic sigh,
As life returns with every cry.
Each silhouette casts reflections deep,
Of those who dream and those who sleep.

So let us wander through this space,
Among reborn trees, find solace and grace.
In every shade, a memory lingers,
Whispering wisdom to hopeful fingers.

Secrets of the Enshrined Roots

Beneath the surface, stories dwell,
Enshrined in roots, they weave and swell.
With every twist, a mystery spins,
Of silent battles and hidden sins.

In the quiet earth, secrets sleep,
Guarded well where shadows creep.
Nature's vault, both deep and wise,
Holds whispers lost, beneath the skies.

Through tangled fibers, life connects,
Unity found in nature's specs.
A network vast, unseen but true,
Binding the past to what is new.

The pulses of the ground resound,
Echoes of life beneath the mound.
With every root, a promise made,
For every shade that must not fade.

So let us kneel and listen near,
Embrace the secrets we hold dear.
For in the roots, the heartbeats lie,
A testament to those who try.

The Song of the Ashen Grove

In the heart of night, a melody hums,
A song of ash, where the stillness drums.
Each note drifts soft on the breeze,
Carried forth by whispering trees.

With every sound, the stillness breaks,
Resonating through the woods it wakes.
An ancient call, with beauty rife,
Echoes of nature, a hymn of life.

The ashen leaves softly sway,
In harmony with the moon's gray ray.
Their subtle dance speaks of the past,
In every rustle, memories cast.

From embers cold, a spirit roams,
In the grove, the lost find homes.
The chorus builds, a world anew,
An orchestra, both wild and true.

So linger here, where the shadows play,
In the ashen grove, let your heart stray.
For every song is a story told,
Of resilience found in ashes bold.

Heartbeat of the Forest Flame

In the heart of the forest, whispers breathe,
Where shadows dance and spirits grieve.
A flicker of light through the emerald shade,
A warm embrace where dreams are made.

The trees hold stories, ancient and wise,
Their branches stretch towards the skies.
A pulse of life, a vibrant beat,
In every leaf, the past we meet.

The brook hums softly, a gentle song,
Carrying secrets where they belong.
Amidst the murmurs, a symphony swells,
Of heartbeats echoing, enchanting spells.

As twilight falls, the fireflies gleam,
Illuminating the paths of a dream.
With every flicker, a tale unfurls,
In the forest's embrace, the magic swirls.

So listen closely, let your heart align,
With the heartbeat of the forest, divine.
For within this realm, you'll find your way,
Where the flame of wonder shall forever stay.

Secrets Hidden in Sylvan Heights

Beyond the meadows, where wildflowers sway,
In sylvan heights, the secrets lay.
Whispered thoughts of the ancients passed,
In every breeze, a memory cast.

The thicket conceals a world anew,
With glimmers of magic, pure and true.
Among the leaves, a story breathes,
A lingering echo, a heart that believes.

With footsteps gentle, tread the ground,
For in each shadow, enchantments abound.
Unearth the wonders lost in time,
Where laughter mingles with the chime.

The moonlit path leads the way,
With silver beams that softly play.
As night descends, the stars ignite,
Guiding the lost with twinkling light.

So venture forth, seek and find,
The secrets hidden, intertwined.
In sylvan heights, let your spirit soar,
For within those woods, magic's heart shall roar.

Tales of the Whispering Woodlands

In the whispering woodlands, stories lie,
Of spirits who dance beneath the sky.
With each rustle of leaves, a tale unfolds,
A legacy passed through the ages, bold.

The brook babbles softly, a tune sincere,
Calling forth dreams, holding them dear.
Echoes of laughter, the wind carries home,
In each gentle breeze, we are never alone.

The midnight owl hoots a timeless ballad,
Sharing the secrets both gentle and valid.
In the depths of the trees, enchantments bloom,
Filling the night with a magical tune.

As dawn breaks softly, the world awakens,
With whispers of hope, no heart is forsaken.
So gather your dreams in the golden light,
And let the woodlands guide you, take flight.

For in these woods, with their tales so bright,
You'll find your way through the darkest night.
With every heartbeat, the stories persist,
In the whispering woodlands, magic exists.

The Resurgence of Timeless Roots

Deep in the earth, where the ancients sleep,
Timeless roots in silence keep.
Through seasons long, their strength is shown,
A legacy of life that's deeply sown.

As the seasons change, a whisper flows,
Through the mayhem of growth, love always shows.
In blooms and boughs, a promise renewed,
Of hope arising, in colors imbued.

The saplings reach for the sunlit skies,
With dreams of tomorrow, the heart defies.
While time marches on, the cycle remains,
In the turn of the leaves, life entertains.

From the roots to the crowns, life's dance will start,
With every new shoot, a beating heart.
So dance with the wind, let your spirit arise,
For in nature's embrace, your true self lies.

Embrace the resurgence, the life that it brings,
In the tapestry woven by magical strings.
For timeless roots hold the essence of grace,
In the dance of existence, we find our place.

Rebirth in the Forest's Whisper

In the heart where shadows play,
Amongst the trees, so green, so gay,
New blooms awaken with morning's light,
Whispers of magic take their flight.

Soft moss blankets the earthen floor,
Ancient secrets, tales of yore,
A gentle breeze, a fleeting sigh,
Promises made beneath the sky.

Hushed voices echo through the leaves,
Each rustle a song that believes,
Life's cycle spins, both harsh and fair,
In whispers of hope, we dare to care.

The brook hums softly, a lullaby,
To seeds of dreams that long to fly,
Rebirth nourished by the sun,
In the forest's heart, all is one.

Time's breath weaves a tapestry bright,
In this realm bathed in golden light,
A sanctuary for souls to mend,
In nature's arms, life finds its end.

In the Shadow of Gentle Flames

Beneath the stars, a flickering glow,
In the hearth's warmth, secrets flow,
Stories spoken of olden dreams,
In the night, where magic gleams.

Embers whisper in the twilight shade,
Casting shadows where spirits wade,
Dancing flames tell tales of might,
Of heroes forged in darkest night.

A crackling laugh, a heartfelt tear,
All are welcome, far or near,
In this circle, bonds are cast,
In the flicker of flames, futures vast.

As the fire wraps the world in grace,
Time slows down in this sacred space,
In the shadows of gentle flames,
We kindle hope and weave our names.

Burning bright through storms that call,
In the warmth, we rise, we fall,
Together united, we shall reclaim,
Our spirits flicker in love's embrace.

The Legacy of the Celestial Pines

Towering heights where eagles soar,
Beneath the boughs, legends roar,
Celestial giants, wise and old,
In their shadows, mysteries unfold.

Roots entwined in the earth's own heart,
Whispering tales, each a part,
Of ancient fables born in dusk,
In the pines, we find our trust.

Time weaves through every knot and bend,
A legacy that will not end,
Branches stretch to touch the sky,
In the woodlands, our dreams can fly.

Through seasons' change, the pines stand tall,
Guardians of echoes, they hear our call,
Their silhouettes in the soft moonlight,
Mark the tales of day and night.

In every leaf, a memory lies,
A sacred bond that never dies,
The legacy crafted by time's gentle hands,
In the whispers of pines, forever stands.

Dawn in a Smoky Glade

Morning breaks with a tender hue,
In the glade where memories brew,
Fog dances softly on dewy grass,
As night's sweet shadows slowly pass.

Golden rays through branches weave,
Awakening dreams that we believe,
Nature's brushstrokes paint the scene,
A canvas alive, divinely serene.

Birds greet the morn with vibrant cheer,
While whispers of the night disappear,
In this soft light, all feels right,
As shadows give way to pure delight.

Each breath infused with life anew,
In the glade, where wishes grew,
A promise murmured with every dawn,
A tapestry of hope, gently drawn.

In this smoky haven, hearts unite,
With every dawn, we take our flight,
To dance beneath the endless skies,
As the world awakens and love replies.

Treetop Reflections of a Burning Past

In the canopies high, shadows play,
Memories linger of a bygone day.
Leaves whisper secrets to the breeze,
A symphony sings beneath the trees.

Embers dance in the twilight glow,
Echoes of flames from long ago.
Branches, like fingers, stretch and sway,
Holding the tales of the forest's fray.

Amidst the silence, the memories swell,
Each rustle a part of a larger spell.
Time weaves through the roots and ground,
In whispers of ash, the past is found.

As twilight falls, a new tale starts,
With each flicker, the forest's heart.
Eternal cycles of loss and gain,
In the tapestry woven through sun and rain.

So let us listen, let us heed,
The lessons of time, the heart's deep need.
For in the shadows, glimmers rest,
Reflections of pasts forever blessed.

Rustling Leaves of Change

A wind stirs softly through the glade,
Whispers of change in the leafy shade.
Golden hues dance on emerald thighs,
As autumn's breath begins to rise.

The branches tremble, a gentle sigh,
Stirring beneath the open sky.
Simple shifts, a fleeting glance,
In nature's rhythm, we find our chance.

With each rustle, a promise lies,
To shed the old and embrace the wise.
In the turning leaves, stories spun,
The cycle of life has just begun.

A tapestry vibrant, colors bright,
In the fading day and the approaching night.
Hope is born with each golden leaf,
As transformations find their belief.

So let the wind carry us away,
Through rustling leaves where dreams may play.
In the heart of the forest, we find our way,
For change is a song, both sweet and fey.

The Forest's Fiery Resurrection

From ashes rise the ancient trees,
In vibrant hues kissed by the breeze.
A spark of life ignites anew,
As dawn breaks forth with every hue.

Flames that once devoured, now turn to gold,
Each leaf a story, each branch a fold.
Resilience sung by softest breeze,
In every whisper, the forest frees.

The earth rejoices, life restores,
From charred remnants, the bloom implores.
New beginnings in shadows cast,
A testament forged from the past.

Soaring high, the birds return,
In the warmth of the sun, all hearts learn.
To rise again from the darkest night,
In the forest's arms, we find our light.

With vibrant colors that paint the air,
The tales of rebirth in moments rare.
The forest speaks in a voice profound,
Of fiery change from the underground.

Bursting Into New Life

In the cradle of earth, seeds await,
A promise of life in the hands of fate.
With a gentle push from the warming sun,
Every bud fulfills what's begun.

Tender shoots stretch towards the sky,
In hues of green, they dare to fly.
Each flower a beacon, bright and bold,
A story of life in colors told.

Beneath the soil, a world abounds,
Whispering secrets in subtle sounds.
Roots intertwine, forming their lace,
Binding all life in a warm embrace.

The forest awakens, the chorus grows,
In every nook, new wonder flows.
Every petal, every leaf,
Reflect the joy of shared belief.

So let us celebrate this sacred space,
Where life bursts forth in every place.
In the heart of the trees, dreams take flight,
In the dance of existence, we find our light.